Michel de Verteuil CSSp

Praying th   ~~pels~~
of Lent
Year B

the columba press

First published in 2000 by
the columba press
55A Spruce Avenue, Stillorgan Industrial Park,
Blackrock, Co Dublin

Cover by Bill Bolger
Origination by The Columba Press
Printed in Ireland by Colour Books Ltd, Dublin

ISBN 1 85607 286 X

Contents

The Method of Lectio Divina

The prayers proposed here are the fruit of *Lectio Divina,* a method of meditative bible reading which goes back to the early centuries of our church, and continues to be a source of deep spiritual growth.

Lectio Divina (a Latin expression which means Sacred Reading) is done in three stages:
Reading: You read the passage slowly and reverentially, allowing the words to sink into your consciousness. If necessary you clarify the meaning of words or expressions that you are not familiar with.
Meditation: You allow the passage to stir up memories within you so that you recognise in it your own experience or that of people who have touched your life.
Prayer: You allow the meditation to lead you to prayer – thanksgiving, humility and petition.

The prayers given here are models. You can use them as they are but they will also suggest ways in which you can pray from your own meditations; you will then be practising *Lectio Divina.*

Now and then the prayers are preceded by quotations from well-known thinkers or spiritual writers. The quotations are there to remind us that through bible reading we enter into the wisdom of humanity.

We practice *Lectio Divina* most fruitfully when we do it in conjunction with the church's Sunday lectionary, spending the week with the gospel passage for the Sunday following. By doing this our personal prayer life becomes integrated into the prayer of the church, and reaches its high point each Sunday in the parish liturgy.

First Sunday

Gospel Reading: Mk 1:12-15
12 The Spirit drove Jesus out into the wilderness and 13he re-mained there for forty days, and was tempted by Satan. He was with the wild beasts, and the angels looked after him.
14After John had been arrested, Jesus went into Galilee. 15There he proclaimed the Good News from God. 'The time has come,' he said, 'and the kingdom of God is close at hand. Repent, and be-lieve the Good News.'

Meditation

St Mark's account of the temptation in the wilderness is very short, just two verses, and so this year the church has added two verses which gives us the option of meditating on a sec-ond moment in the life of Jesus, the beginning of his public ministry.

Verses 12-13: To 'tempt' in the bible means to test or, more precisely, to purify through an ordeal, 'like gold in the furnace' (Wis 3:6). Our text is saying that Satan gave Jesus a good shaking up, just as God allowed him to 'test' Job in the Old Testament story (Job 1 and 2).

Psalm 22:12-13 & 15-16 explains the meaning of 'He was with the wild beasts'. In this terrible situation God was keep-ing a watchful eye on Jesus making sure that no harm came to him. Deuteronomy 8:2-4, conveys the same meaning.

Verses 14-15 speak of a moment when God comes into the life of an individual or community. St Mark says that at such mo-ments people experience four things:
– a long awaited moment has arrived;

– spiritual growth seems a real possibility;
– people see the error of their ways;
– they feel they can trust this new orientation which their lives have taken.

Gospel Prayer

Lord we pray today for all those whom your Spirit has driven out into the wilderness:
– who have been betrayed by a loved one;
– who have lost their jobs with no hope of getting another;
– who find themselves in prison;
– who have just learnt that they are terminally ill.
The days seem long to them, they feel battered by demons, surrounded by wild beasts.
Lord, send them your angels to look after them.

Lord, we embark on projects easily and confidently:
– a new relationship;
– a leadership role in our community;
– a new movement, a political party.
But the good feeling doesn't last.
Your spirit must drive us out into the wilderness and we must remain there forty long days,
tempted by Satan and surrounded by wild beasts while angels look after us.
Only then are we fit to commit ourselves.

Lord, during the course of the year we turn our eyes to many ugly things about ourselves:
– our meanness and envy;
– the hurts we have not forgiven;
– the desire to take revenge.
During this Lent, let your Spirit drive us into the wilderness and keep us there for forty days,
where we will face up to the demons within us and the wild beasts tearing at us,
knowing all the time that your angels are looking after us.

Lord, we thank you in the name of all those for whom this
Lent will be a season of grace,
when Jesus will come into their lives.
They will know that the moment they were running away
from has finally come,
a life of holiness will seem within their grasp,
they will turn away from their sin and give themselves trust-
ingly to the new vision you have brought them to.

Lord, we thank you for those who continue to work for reconciliation where there is hatred and violence:
– in South Africa, the Middle East, Sri Lanka, Northern
Ireland;
– in work places where workers and employers have no trust;
– where racism divides people.

They are Jesus going into Galilee after John had been arrested,
proclaiming:
– that it is a moment not of despair but of grace;
– that love and harmony are real options;
– that people can put their trust in the victory of good over
evil.

Second Sunday

Gospel Reading: Mk 9:2-10
2Jesus took with him Peter and James and John and led them up a high mountain where they could be alone by themselves. There in their presence he was transfigured: 3his clothes became dazzlingly white, whiter than any earthly bleacher could make them. 4Elijah appeared to them with Moses; and they were talking with Jesus.
5Then Peter spoke to Jesus. 'Rabbi', he said 'it is wonderful for us to be here; so let us make three tents, one for you, one for Moses and one for Elijah.' 6He did not know what to say; they were so frightened. 7And a cloud came, covering them in shadow; and there came a voice from the cloud, 'This is my Son, the Beloved. Listen to him.' 8Then suddenly, when they looked round, they saw no one with them any more but only Jesus.
9As they came down the mountain he warned them to tell no one what they had seen, until after the Son of Man had risen from the dead. 10They observed the warning faithfully, though among themselves they discussed what 'rising from the dead' could mean.

Meditation

Notice that though we usually refer to this story as the transfiguration, Jesus' appearing in glory was only one stage in a journey the apostles made in their relationship with him. We can distinguish *five* such stages and you can recognise them all in your meditation.

Verse 2: the high mountain is a symbol of the painful journey the apostles must make with Jesus before he can be transfigured in their presence.

Verses 3 to 6: the glory of Jesus is beyond the capacity of any earthly power, it is from God alone. Note St Mark's comment on why St Peter proposed building three tents: he was desperately afraid of losing the moment.

Verse 7: the relationship with Jesus is covered by a cloud and yet it is from within the cloud that they experience a renewed commitment to Jesus.

Verse 8: the apostles are alone with Jesus and they come down the mountain together.

Verses 9 to 10: it is only when they have seen Jesus die and rise from the dead that the apostles will understand the full significance of the experience.

Gospel Prayer

Lord, we thank you for the transfiguration experiences that you will favour your people with during this Lent:
– a Bible passage will suddenly become deep and enriching for us;
– during a parish mission we will feel the power of the message of Jesus;
– we will celebrate a liturgy that fills us with consolation.
At that moment we will experience a glory that is not from this earth and we will cry out that it is wonderful for us to be here.

Lord, we don't take time to know the people we live with:
– either we are too busy with our own affairs;
– or we judge others by their appearances, how they dress, what they have achieved.
If only we let them lead us up a high mountain where we can be alone by ourselves,
they can be transfigured in our presence and we will see the glory that is within them and comes from you.
Lord, we thank you for the long journey we have made with our spouse, our closest friend.

We remember the day when they first appeared glorious to us, with a glory we had never though possible.

We found it wonderful that we should be together, in fact so wonderful that we were afraid of losing the moment.

We know now that a relationship cannot remain there.

So a dark cloud came over and covered the relationship with a shadow.

But within the very insecurity of that time we discovered that this was your beloved whom we wanted to commit ourselves to forever.

Shortly afterwards the relationship was stable again and we came down the mountain together.

But we knew in some vague way that we would have to live through many deaths and resurrections before we could understand the journey we had made.

Lord, we ask you to send wise spiritual guides to your church, who will help us grow in our relationship with you:
– who will encourage us to let ourselves be led up the high mountain you call us to;
– who will be part of the transfiguration experience, conversing with Jesus like Moses or Elijah;
– who will stay with us when the cloud comes and covers us in shadows;
– and who will warn us that we must not speak of these things until we have seen the Son of Man rise from the dead.

Lord, we pray today for those who have committed themselves to a noble cause,
help them to move freely beyond the first experience of joy and excitement,
to remain with their commitment when a cloud comes and covers them in shadow,
for it is from the cloud that they will learn for sure that it is your work they have given themselves to and they can find you in it.

Lord, from time to time, you give us beautiful experiences, moments which bind us to a person or a cause.

But it is only when we have come down from the mountain and see that person or cause die and rise from the dead, that we will be able to speak about what happened on the mountain.

Third Sunday

Gospel Reading: John 2:13-25
[13] Just before the Jewish Passover Jesus went up to Jerusalem, [14] and in the Temple he found people selling cattle and sheep and pigeons, and the money changers sitting at their counters there. [15] Making a whip out of some cord, he drove them all out of the Temple, cattle and sheep as well, scattered the money changers' coins, knocked their tables over [16] and said to the pigeon-sellers, 'Take all this out of here and stop turning my Father's house into a market.' [17] Then his disciples remembered the words of scripture: Zeal for your house will devour me. [18] The Jews intervened and said, 'What sign can you show us to justify what you have done?' [19] Jesus answered, 'Destroy this sanctuary, and in three days I will raise it up.' [20] The Jews replied, 'It has taken forty-six years to build this sanctuary: are you going to raise it up in three days?' [21] But he was speaking of the sanctuary that was his body, [22] and when Jesus rose from the dead, his disciples remembered that he had said this, and they believed the scripture and the words he had said.
[23] During his stay in Jerusalem for the Passover many believed in his name when they saw the signs that he gave, [24] but Jesus knew them all and did not trust himself to them; [25] he never needed evidence about any man; he could tell what a man had in him.

Meditation

This Sunday we have John's account of the cleansing of the temple. The passage is in *three* sections:
– *verses 13-17:* the cleansing;
– *verses 18-22:* the dialogue between Jesus and Jews;
– *verses 23-25:* a comment on Jesus' attitude towards people.
Note carefully Jesus' complaint against the vendors.

Three questions to ask yourself:
1. What are the temples that people turn into market places today?
2. Why is Jesus cleansing these temples?
3. How is he doing it?

Identify with what John calls the 'zeal' of Jesus; we accept so easily the profanation of temples; for him it is totally unacceptable.

In the dialogue between Jesus and the Jews identify the opposed mentalities; the Jews are concerned with the sanctuary which takes forty-six years to build and its destruction is a disaster; Jesus' concern is for the kind that can always be rebuilt in three days.

Verse 22: it is only when we have experienced death/resurrection that we understand certain lessons of life.

Jesus' reserve when he meets popularity *(Verses 23 to 25)* is a model for the church and for us as individuals.

Gospel Prayer

Lord, there are so many temples that people are turning into market places today:
– children are a sacred trust, but we project our own ambitions and our hurts on them;
– our relationship with our spouse we turn into a battlefield where we make sure to occupy the higher ground;
– we enter into friendship to get advantages for ourselves;
– the land we see as a source of easy profit;
– the human body we treat as an object of competitions;
– a church community becomes a place for prestige and power.

We thank you for the times you sent Jesus into those temples,
he made a whip out of some cord and drove us out,
scattering our coins and knocking our counting tables over.
We were angry, hurt and confused,
but looking back now we recognise that it was zeal for your
house which devoured you.

Lord, there was a time when we had made our relationship
with you a matter of rewards for good works,
we complained that you let us suffer, that you left our
prayers unanswered, that others we considered less
virtuous than ourselves were more blessed than we were.
But all the time it was Jesus cleansing your house,
driving away the baggage of the market place
so that we could come to you in humble adoration and trust.

Lord, forgive us that we are no longer indignant when
sacred places are being violated.

We thank you for those whom zeal for your house has devoured:
– Martin Luther King overturning the segregation
counters in the Southern United States;
– Steve Biko communicating a sense of self-worth to his fel-
low South Africans;
– labour leaders here at home who brought dignity to workers.

Lord, we are always fearful of losing what is secondary to your
church,
large numbers, popularity, the patronage of the powerful,
fearful that what has taken forty-six years to build might be
destroyed.
As a result we compromise and tolerate and remain passive.
Remind us, Lord, that the only sanctuary that counts is the
body of Jesus, his love, his solidarity with the poor and the
oppressed,
and once we are truly his body in our society we can rebuild
in three days whatever earthly powers destroy.

Lord, there are so many deep lessons about life that we learnt from our parents and grandparents,
but it is only after we have passed through resurrection from the dead that we remember what they taught us and we believe the words they said.

Lord, be with you church in our moments of success, when many believe in us because they see signs we give, our schools and other institutions, our lively liturgies and our rallies.
Remind us what people have in them so that we may not put our trust in their approval but only in our fidelity to you.

Fourth Sunday

Gospel Reading: Jn 3:14-21
Jesus said to Nicodemus:
[14]'The Son of Man must be lifted up
as Moses lifted up the serpent in the desert,
[15]so that everyone who believes may have eternal life in him.
[16]Yes, God loved the world so much
that he gave his only Son,
so that everyone who believes in him may not be lost
but may have eternal life.
[17]For God sent his Son into the world
not to condemn the world,
but so that through him the world might be saved.
[18]No one who believes in him will be condemned;
but whoever refuses to believe is condemned already,
because he has refused to believe
in the name of God's only Son.
[19]On these ground is sentence pronounced:
that though the light has come into the world
men have shown they prefer
darkness to the light
because their deeds were evil.
[20]And indeed, everybody who does wrong hates the light and
avoids it,
for fear his actions should be exposed;
[21]but the man who lives by the truth
comes out into the light,
so that it may be plainly seen that what he does is done in God.'

Meditation

You will notice that certain themes run through the passage, expressed in various metaphors and with various emphases. John is like a steelband arranger working out variations on his tune for panorama. Take the passage slowly, one section at a time.

In *verses 13 to 15* the theme is the necessity for the Son of Man to be lifted up if he is to be a source of life for his followers. St John adds a variation by remembering the serpent in the desert, the symbol of death turned into a source of life.

In *verse 16* there are *two* movements:
1. God's love expressed practically in his giving what is most precious to him.
2. The motive for (as well as the actual fruit of) this love expressed in the two possible outcomes for people, being lost on the one hand and having eternal life on the other.

Verse 17 brings back the teaching of the previous verse through the metaphors of condemning and being saved.

Verse 18 brings back the metaphor of being condemned and links it to the option of believing in love or not believing.

In *verse 19* Jesus reflects on how people are condemned; the only valid condemnation is the one which comes from within oneself.

In *verses 20 and 21* the teaching is clarified with an analysis of how we make our choice of darkness or light.

Gospel Prayer

Lord, we would like to be a source of life for others without
cost to ourselves.
We thank you for true leaders we have met, who knew the law
of life as Jesus did,
that we must make ourselves vulnerable, be open to failure
and humiliation, allowing ourselves to be lifted up as
Moses lifted up the serpent in the desert, if our followers
are to find life in us.

Lord, there was a time when we were afraid of death, of
failing, suffering, being rejected by others.
This fear was a bondage for us.
We thank you that you lifted up a Son of Man before us and
invited us to look honestly at those things that frightened us;
we looked on that Son of Man and lived.

Lord, we thank you for all those who love –
parents, grandparents, spouses, community leaders –
they love so much that they give what is most precious to
them,
their careers, their future security, their own friends,
so that those whom they love might experience that they
can trust and so not be lost but live.

Lord, we think today of those in our society who are lost:
– addicts to drugs or alcohol;
– those who are eaten up with bitterness and envy;
– those who cannot forgive.
We remember that your will is that they should not be lost,
for them you gave your only Son;
forgive us that we have not mediated your love to them.

Lord, we pray for teachers
in schools, church communities, families.

Remind them that you have sent them into their
communities not to condemn but so that through them their
charges might be saved.

Lord, there is nothing more terrible in life than to feel condemned:
– to living without purpose;
– to experiencing failure and rejection whatever happens;
– to knowing that you will never be admired by others;
and the root of it is not believing that you are loved.
Help us to be the presence of your only Son in the world, so
that people might not go through life condemned.

Lord, we pray for your church that we may never give in to
the tendency to condemn.
Help us to focus on being true to you so that others may
come to us not from fear of being condemned but from the
truth that is in themselves.

Lord, we thank you for the journey to grace that many of us
have made during this Lent.
For many years you were calling us, inviting us to look honestly at our addictions, our vanity, our envy.
We hated the light, avoided it for fear that the truth about
ourselves should be exposed.
During these days we were brought to look at ourselves and
came out into the light, feeling inner peace because we knew
that what we were doing, we were doing in you.

Fifth Sunday

Gospel Reading: Jn 12:20-33

20Among those who went up to worship at the festival were some Greeks. 21These approached Philip, who came from Bethsaida in Galilee, and put this request to him, 'Sir, we should like to see Jesus.' 22Philip went to tell Andrew, and Andrew and Philip together went to tell Jesus. 23Jesus replied to them:

'Now the hour has come
for the Son of Man to be glorified.
24I tell you, most solemnly,
unless a wheat grain falls on the ground and dies,
it remains only a single grain;
but if it dies,
it yields a rich harvest.
25Anyone who loves his life loses it;
anyone who hates his life in this world
will keep it for the eternal life.
26If a man serves me, he must follow me,
wherever I am, my servant will be there too.
If anyone serves me, my Father will honour him.
27Now my soul is troubled.
What shall I say:
Father, save me from this hour?
But it was for this very reason that I have come to this hour.
28Father, glorify your name!'
A voice came from heaven, 'I have glorified it, and I will glorify it again.'
29People standing by, who heard this, said it was a clap of thunder; others said, 'It was an angel speaking to him.' 30Jesus answered, 'It was not for my sake that this voice came, but for yours.
31Now sentence is being passed on this world;
now the prince of this world is to be overthrown.
32And when I am lifted up from the earth,
I shall draw all men to myself.'
33By these words he indicated the kind of death he would die.

Meditation

Verse 23 shows us Jesus fully conscious of where he is; the 'hour' is the kind of crisis moment that occurs just once or twice in a lifetime.

Verse 24 is a very brief parable. Feel the pain implied in 'falls on the ground and dies'. Stay with possible outcomes of the hour: remaining only a single grain on the one hand and yielding rich harvest on the other.

Verse 25 is the same teaching but the contrast is between clinging to the present and losing what one has, and the contrary, risking the present with the effect of saving the future. Identify with both possibilities, one tragic, the other glorious.

Verse 26 makes the teaching personal: Jesus himself made the journey of faith.

As a follow up, *verse 27* invites us to accompany Jesus as he makes his journey. We have here John's account of the agony in the garden, the painful movement from 'save me from this hour' to 'Father, glorify your name', which is the first petition of the Our Father and in biblical language means the same as the third petition, 'your will be done'.

In *verses 28 to 30* the bystanders are given the opportunity to witness Jesus' journey.

Verses 31 and 32 expresses the attitude of Jesus as he faces his hour. There is no self-pity, no bitterness, he is confident that God's work will be done through him.

Gospel Prayer

Lord, we remember today all those who know that the hour
has come for them:
– couples about to commit themselves to each other for life;
– people, secure in their jobs, who know you are calling them
to move into some new field;
– church communities getting involved in social issues;
– parents who must now let go of their children;
– friends who have decided to break off a relationship which
is harmful to them;
– families facing a drop in their standard of living.
Help them to feel Jesus making the journey with them.
Remind them of his pain and how he had to tell himself that
unless the grain of wheat falls on the ground and dies it remains only a single grain, but if it dies it yields a rich harvest.

Lord, we thank you that the church in many countries has
taken the risk of falling on the ground and dying:
– has lost the support of the powerful and the wealthy by em-
bracing the cause of the poor;
– has preached ideals of chastity in societies that are permis-
sive;
– has allowed little people to follow their own pace and to
make mistakes.
And now it is yielding a rich harvest.

Lord, as we look back on our lives we remember how we did
not take the risks we should have and so have remained a single grain instead of yielding a rich harvest.

Help us to live with our mistakes, to give up our regrets,
letting them fall on the ground and die,
trusting that there is another kind of harvest that we can yield.

Lord, the first priority for the wealthy nations of the world
today is to preserve their wealth.
We thank you for the prophetic voices that have been speak-

ing out, reminding these nations of the message of Jesus,
that if they remain turned in on their worldly possessions they
will lose them all,
whereas if they take the risk of sharing with others they will
experience peace and security for the future.

Lord, we who are in positions of authority over others –
parents, teachers, priest, community leaders –
we like to prescribe things for others,
handing on abstract teachings on right and wrong.
Remind us that we can only share our own journeys,
inviting others to follow us so that where we are they may be
there too,
and leaving it up to you to honour them.

Lord, we think today of those whose souls are troubled as they
meet their hour:
– activists facing imprisonment or even death;
– priests and religious suddenly confronted with the implica-
tions of their vows;
– church leaders as they face up to the frustrations of acting
democratically.
We feel for them as in their confusion they ask you, 'What
shall I say? Father save me from this hour.'
Give them the faith to see that it was for this very reason that
they have come to this hour and to invite you to glorify your
name.

Palm Sunday
Procession of Palms

Reading Mk 11:1-10
¹When they were approaching Jerusalem, in sight of Bethphage and Bethany, close by the Mount of Olives, Jesus sent two of his disciples ²and said to them, 'Go off to the village facing you, and as soon as you enter it you will find a tethered colt that no one has yet ridden. Untie it and bring it here. ³If anyone says to you, "What are you doing?" say, "The Master needs it and will send it back directly."' ⁴They went off and found a colt tethered near a door in the open street. As they untied it, ⁵some men standing there said, 'What are you doing, untying that colt?' ⁶They gave the answer Jesus had told them, and the men let them go. ⁷Then they took the colt to Jesus and threw their cloaks on its back, and he sat on it. ⁸Many people spread their cloaks on the road, others greenery which they had cut in the fields. ⁹And those who went in front and those who followed were all shouting, 'Hosanna! Blessings on him who comes in the name of the Lord! ¹⁰Blessings on the coming kingdom of our father David! Hosanna in the highest heavens!'

Meditation

The gospel reading for the procession of palms is quite naturally the story of Jesus' entry into Jerusalem, Mark's account since this is Mark's year. Do not allow the other accounts to influence your meditation; focus exclusively on the text before you.

Mark's account is in *two* stages:
Verses 1-6 set the stage for the main story. You might like to stay with these verses, noticing how Jesus' entry into Jerusalem was well planned; he was able to call on the help of friends he had in the city so that he could make his symbolic entry on a donkey.

The story told in *verses 7-9* is all symbolic. Three Old Testament texts will help you enter into the symbolism:

– Zachariah 9:9-10, which is not referred to explicitly as it is in some of the other accounts but was clearly in the mind of Jesus himself. St Mark emphasises his regal bearings as he sat on the donkey.

– Psalm 118 is quoted in *verses 9 and 10*. This psalm celebrates the victory of one who by God's grace has triumphed over all obstacles. How was the entry of Jesus into Jerusalem such a triumph?

– 2 Samuel 7:16 promises that the kingdom of David will be established for ever. In what way did Jesus' entry give the assurance that this promise would soon be fulfilled?

Gospel Prayer

Lord, often we think that because we are working for a good cause we can act in a slipshod way.
We thank you for the example of Jesus, how he planned carefully his entry into Jerusalem, availing himself of the help his friends in the city could give him.
We thank you for well-organised leaders like him.
When we work with them, we find like Jesus' disciples that things turn out as we are told, and we are let go to do what we have to.

Lord, we remember today those who choose consciously to remain compassionate in the face of hostility:
– parents having to relate with rebellious teenagers;
– lay readers criticised unfairly in the parish community;
– those who protest non-violently against injustice;
– immigrants keeping their dignity when they are subject to racial slurs.
They are like Jesus when he approached Jerusalem and made

it quite clear that he would banish the bow of war and pro-claim a universal empire of peace.

Lord, our world is dominated by powerful people who put their trust in prestige, wealth or military might, so that we have lost hope and become cynical.
We long for leaders who are different, imitators of Jesus who will choose like him the way of humility and truth,
taking away our apathy so that we will be moved to shout,
'Hosanna, Blessings on him who comes in the name of the Lord,'
taking away despair so that we hope again in the coming kingdom of our father David.

Lord, we pray that as we enter Holy Week we may renew our faith in the values of Jesus,
bring out our festive branches to welcome him, and shout aloud, 'blessings on him who comes in the name of the Lord.'

Lord, we thank you for those brief moments when we experi-ence deep joy:
– prayer experiences when everything in life comes together;
– fervent parish liturgies;
– times of intimacy between spouses or friends;
– a social moment emerges which fills us with hope.
At those times we know that you are entering our lives as Jesus entered Jerusalem.
It is a time of freshness and greenery.
We sense that a coming of your kingdom is immanent and shout, 'Hosanna in the highest heavens.'
Thank you, Lord.

Palm Sunday
The Passion

The gospel reading is the entire story of the passion according to St Mark. We suggest that you focus on the last section, *Mk 15:21-41*.

Reading Mk 15:21-41

21 They enlisted a passer-by, Simon of Cyrene, father of Alexander and Rufus, who was coming in from the country, to carry his cross. 22 They brought Jesus to the place called Golgotha, which means the place of the skull. 23 They offered him wine mixed with myrrh, but he refused it. 24 Then they crucified him, and shared out his clothing, casting lots to decide what each should get. 25 It was the third hour when they crucified him. 26 The inscription giving the charge against him read: 'The King of the Jews.' 27 And they crucified two robbers with him, one on his right, and one on his left. 29 The passers-by jeered at him; they shook their heads and said, 'Aha! So you would destroy the Temple and rebuild it in three days! 30 Then save yourself: come down from the cross!' 31 The chief priests and the scribes mocked him among themselves in the same way. They said, 'He saved others, he cannot save himself. 32 Let the Christ, the king of Israel, come down from the cross now, for us to see it and believe.' Even those who were crucified with him taunted him.

33 When the sixth hour came there was darkness over the whole land until the ninth hour. 34 And at the ninth hour Jesus cried out in a loud voice, 'Eloi, Eloi, lama sabachthani?' This means 'My God, my God, why have you deserted me?' 35 When some of those who stood by heard this, they said, 'Listen, he is calling on Elijah.' 36 Someone ran and soaked a sponge in vinegar and, putting it on a reed, gave it him to drink, saying, 'Wait and see if Elijah will come to take him down.' 37 But Jesus gave a loud cry and breathed his last. 38 And the veil of the Temple was torn in two from top to bottom. 39 The centurion, who was standing in front of him, had seen how he had died, and he said, 'In truth this man was a son of God.'

40 There were some women watching from a distance. Among them were Mary of Magdala, Mary who was the mother of James the younger, and Joset, and Salome. 41 These used to follow him and look after him when he was in Galilee. And there were many other women there who had come up to Jerusalem with him.

Meditation

The story is easily divided, each section giving one incident in these last hours of the earthly life of Jesus.

Verse 21: The three synoptic gospels (contrary to St John's account) speak of this person who was made to carry the cross and Christians have always seen in him the symbol of their vocation to share in the sufferings of Jesus.

Verse 22: All the gospel accounts note the name of the place where Jesus was crucified, the synoptics giving the meaning which is highly symbolic.

Verses 23-27: Mark's account of the actual crucifixion is extremely simple, almost as if the reality was too painful to dwell on.

Verses 29-32: (Note that there is no verse 28). It is important to note that for the gospel writers the mocking of Jesus is more significant than the physical pain of the crucifixion. The charge that he 'saved others but could not save himself' is of course perfectly true although not in the sense that his accusers made it.

Verses 33-36 describe the last moments. It is useful to read Psalm 22 (21 in the Psalter) to get the deep significance of the cry of Jesus. Hebrews 5:7 will also help your meditations on this section.

Verses 37-39: the death of Jesus. The act of faith of the centurion is the intended climax of the whole gospel of Mark.

Verses 40-41 introduce the faithful women, some of whom will be at the tomb on Easter Sunday morning. It is surely significant that, according to Mark, only women remained faithful to the end.

Gospel Prayer

Lord, we thank you for those precious moments when you allowed us to experience that we played a significant part in your work of grace:
– we were there when a holy person was dying and said the final prayers;
– a national crisis arose, we were in the right place and did our duty to the country;
– members of our community shared their sorrows with us;
– we were at prayer and suddenly felt our solidarity with the suffering of the world.
It was a fleeting moment but the memory remains.
It must have been like that for Simon of Cyrene when he happened to be passing by, coming in from the country, and they enlisted him to carry the cross of Jesus.
Thank you, Lord.

Lord, you often make a place of death the source of new life:
– we were abandoned by our friends but learnt how deep our inner resources were;
– a parent died and the family came together as never before.
You teach us that you always bring life, and this is why your Son Jesus was not afraid when they brought him to a place called Golgotha, which means the place of the skull.

Lord, we thank you for the members of our church who are not afraid to be associated with those whom society labels disreputable:
– those who work with AIDS patients;
– movements like St Vincent de Paul and the Legion of Mary;
– priest-workers.
Often they are criticised and mocked but we see in them Jesus crucified with two robbers, one on his right and the other on his left. Like him it can be rightly said that their only interest is in saving others, they are not unduly concerned with saving themselves.

'It was essential that Jesus should become completely like his brothers so that he could be a compassionate and trustworthy high priest of God's religion.' – Heb 2:17
Lord, people sometimes think that because we are leaders in the church we must always be calm and composed.
We thank you for teaching us that when you yourself seem to be silent,
we can cry in a loud voice, 'My God, my God, why have you deserted me?'

'To destroy human power nothing more is required than to be indifferent to its threats and to prefer other goods to those which it promises.' – R. H. Tawney
Lord, how true it is that success or popularity is not really important in life. The only important thing is that some unbelieving centurion, seeing how we live and die, could say, 'in truth this was a son of God'.

Lord, when great people remain faithful unto death,
showing no anger or resentment to their enemies
but on the contrary continuing to love and forgive,
it shows us how false are the barriers we set up to separate
people into bad and good; the veils we have erected in your
temple are torn in two from top to bottom.

'Many Catholics resent the bishops holding the uncomfortable truth because it disturbs their privilege and security.' – Capetown Archdiocesan Justice and Peace Commission, July 1990

Lord, we thank you for faithful followers of Jesus,

those who like the women in the gospel look after him in Galilee where it is safe and then come up to Jerusalem with him even though it is dangerous and are there watching with him as he hangs on the cross.

Sacred Triduum

Introduction

On Holy Thursday evening the church comes to the end of the lenten season and enters the Sacred Triduum, which concludes with the Vigil and the Mass of the Resurrection on the night of Holy Saturday.

The Sacred Triduum, as the name implies, is one three-day celebration, a point to be stressed since in recent centuries Holy Thursday, Good Friday and Holy Saturday were considered to be three distinct celebrations.

The Triduum celebrates Jesus' victory. Contrary to appearances, sin and death did not conquer him; he conquered them through the power of the Father, and we all share in his victory.

His weapons of conquest, ours as well as his, are trust in the Father, patience, compassion, forgiveness, summed up in Jn 12:1 as 'love to the end'.

Meditation on the gospels within the church's liturgy remains the most effective way of entering into the spirit of the Triduum.

Holy Thursday

Gospel Reading Jn 13:1-15

[1] It was before the festival of the Passover, and Jesus knew that the hour had come for him to pass from this world to the Father. He had always loved those who were his in the world, but now he showed how perfect his love was.

[2] They were at supper, and the devil had already put it into the mind of Judas Iscariot son of Simon, to betray him. [3] Jesus knew that the Father had put everything into his hands, and that he had come from God and was returning to God, [4] and he got up from table, removed his outer garment and, taking a towel, wrapped it round his waist; [5] he then poured water into a basin and began to wash the disciples' feet and to wipe them with the towel he was wearing.

[6] He came to Simon Peter, who said to him, 'Lord, are you going to wash my feet?' [7] Jesus answered, 'At the moment you do not know what I am doing, but later you will understand.' [8] 'Never!' said Peter 'You shall never wash my feet.' Jesus replied, 'If I do not wash you, you can have nothing in common with me.' [9] 'Then, Lord,' said Simon Peter 'not only my feet, but my hands and my head as well!' [10] Jesus said, 'No one who has taken a bath needs washing, he is clean all over. You too are clean, though not all of you are.' [11] He knew who was going to betray him, that was why he said, 'though not all of you are.'

[12] When he had washed their feet and put on his clothes again he went back to the table. 'Do you understand' he said 'what I have done to you? [13] You call me Master and Lord, and rightly; so I am. [14] If I, then, the Lord and Master, have washed your feet, you should wash each other's feet. [15] I have given you an example so that you may copy what I have done to you.'

Meditation

The Mass of Holy Thursday is the introduction to the Sacred Triduum and the gospel reading for the Mass should be read within that context: just like the story of Jesus' entry into Jerusalem, this passage too gives the key to understanding the whole passion of Jesus.

Verse 1 is the introduction, not merely to the story of the foot-washing but to St John's long account of Jesus' suffering, death and resurrection. If you are meditating on this verse it would be better to adopt the more accurate translation: 'he loved them to the end', an expression which can and should be interpreted at many different levels.

St John has worked several different strands into the story of the foot-washing and it would be important that at any one moment you focus on one only of these:
– Jesus by his action gave the apostles a lesson in true leadership. The point is clearly made in *verses 12 to 15*.
– Jesus was explaining to them the significance of what they would witness over the following three days. This comes out of his statement in *verse 7*, 'at the moment you do not know what I am doing, but later you will understand'.
– His action explained the experience of the sacraments, especially of baptism. This is clear from the symbolism of washing. Today we can include the experience of the sacrament of reconciliation and also of the Eucharist.

You might like to focus on St Peter, entering into the attitude which led to his responses to Jesus and asking yourself what it meant for him to meet someone like Jesus.

Notice too that for St John the whole event is within the framework of a confrontation between Jesus and 'the devil'. You might like to focus on that aspect looking at the kind of power which Jesus exercised. You will certainly find echoes of the Palm Sunday story.

Gospel Prayer

'His state was divine, yet he did not cling to his equality with God but emptied himself to assume the condition of a slave.'

– Phil 2:6-7

Lord, as we enter this Sacred Triduum, when we remember the passion of your Son Jesus,
you explain to us the deep meaning of what happened on Calvary.
Jesus, he who is Lord and master, in whose hands you have left everything created,
renounced whatever could give the impression that he was interested in earthly power,
and showed himself to the world for what he was, a humble servant.
Now that he has returned to his place at your right hand we can understand what he has done for us: we are now clean, so totally clean that we can be indifferent to popularity or success,
since nothing that life brings, neither humiliation nor failure of any kind, can make us unclean,
and even when we sin there remains deep within us a clean place where we can have communion with you.
He has left us an example too, a standard for judging all our actions: are we at the service of one another?

Lord, we thank you for those who remain faithful:
– parents who care for wayward children;
– those who continue to serve in public office in spite of criticism;
– religious who persevere in their vows;
– lay leaders in church communities.
We celebrate them too in this Triduum,
having loved those who were their own in the world,
they loved them to the end.

'One hand can't clap.' – Trinidad saying
Lord, when we are in a position of authority,
in the nation, a parish or our family,
we gradually find our identity in being influential or having others obey us,
but if, like Jesus, we know that whatever we have you have put into our hands,
that we have come from you and are returning to you,
it would cost us nothing to get up from our place of honour,
remove the trappings of authority
and put ourselves at the service of those under us.

'The way to being is the way of non-assertion. It is God's way.'
                                            – Thomas Merton
Lord, the desire to dominate, to understand everything, to remain in control,
these are like the outer garments of ourselves which, like Jesus, we must lay aside
so that we can reverence the people around us.

Lord, pride can take strange forms.
We always like to be in a position of helping others:
– praying for the conversion of sinners;
– wealthy people giving alms to the poor;
– teachers who instruct those who do not know.
If those whom we are helping came to us wanting to be of service, we would respond as Peter did to Jesus, 'never, you shall never wash my feet!'
But how true it is that we cannot enter into communion with someone unless we let that person minister to us.

Lord, we pray for those who will be baptised on Holy Saturday.
Help them to prepare themselves so well for that moment that, having been washed in the font, they may feel totally clean.

Lord, we thank you for the people who have influenced us deeply.
It was not so much what they said but how they related with us.
Like Jesus they gave us an example so that we now copy what they did to us.

Lord, we pray for parents.
So often they must say to their children, 'at the moment you do not know what I am doing, but later you will understand'.

'Here the church is naked but it has the possibility to serve the people. We were for so long powerful and privileged. Now we are but one element of a group contributing to the formation of a just society.' – Catholic Bishops in Cuba
Lord, we thank you that in many countries your church has accepted the need to remove its outer garments of power and privilege, and has taken its place among the other servants of your people.

Good Friday

Gospel Reading Jn 19:17-30

[17]Carrying his own cross he went out of the city to the place of the skull, or, as it was called in Hebrew, Golgotha, [18]where they crucified him with two others, one on either side with Jesus in the middle. [19]Pilate wrote out a notice and had it fixed to the cross; it ran: 'Jesus the Nazarene, King of the Jews.' [20]This notice was read by many of the Jews, because the place where Jesus was crucified was not far from the city, and the writing was in Hebrew, Latin and Greek. [21]So the Jewish chief priests said to Pilate, 'You should not write "'ing of the Jews", but "this man said: I am King of the Jews".' [22]Pilate answered, 'What I have written, I have written.' [23]When the soldiers had finished crucifying Jesus they took his clothing and divided it into four shares, one for each soldier. His undergarment was seamless, woven in one piece from neck to hem; [24]so they said to one another, 'Instead of tearing it, let's throw dice to decide who is to have it.' In this way the words of scripture were fulfilled:

> *They shared out my clothing among them*
> *They cast lots for my clothes.*

[25]This is exactly what the soldiers did.
Near the cross of Jesus stood his mother and his mother's sister, Mary the wife of Clopas, and Mary of Magdala. [26]Seeing his mother and the disciple he loved standing near her, Judas said to his mother, 'Woman, this is your son.' [27]Then to the disciple he said, 'This is your mother.' And from that moment the disciple made a place for her in his home.
[28]After this, Jesus knew that everything had now been completed, and to fulfil the scripture perfectly he said: 'I am thirsty.' [29]A jar full of vinegar stood there, so putting a sponge soaked in vinegar on a hyssop stick they held it up to his mouth. [30]After Jesus had taken the vinegar he said, 'It is accomplished.' And bowing his head he gave up the spirit.

Meditation

I am suggesting that you meditate on one section only of the long gospel reading that is fixed for today's service, *verses 17 to 30*, the final stages of the passion narrative according to St John.

These verses tell of a series of incidents each of which is highly symbolical. It is not always easy to enter into the symbols because St John takes for granted that his readers know the Old Testament and his stories are to be interpreted in the light of certain Old Testament texts. Remember, however, that experience is as safe a guide as scholarship for entering into biblical stories.

St John stresses right through his account of the passion that Jesus was master of his destiny: 'no one takes my life from me, I lay it down of my own free will', he is quoted as saying in chapter 10, verse 18. This is why St John says in *verse 17* that Jesus 'carried his own cross'.

Verse 18 is the fulfilment of Isaiah's prophecy that God's servant would 'let himself be taken for a sinner' (53:12).

The episode in *verses 19 to 22* may seem trivial but for St John it was very significant: the royalty of Jesus is proclaimed in the main languages of the world of that time and even the pagan governor was insistent on proclaiming it.

Verses 23 and 24 are difficult to interpret. They are a fulfilment of Psalm 22, especially verse 18, evoking the humiliation of Jesus. But there is certainly a reference to the garment of the High Priest (Exodus 39:27).

Verses 25 and 26 are verses that are dear to us Catholics since they tell how Mary was designated mother of the disciples of Jesus. Mary can be interpreted as a symbol of the church.

In *verses 28 to 30* the stress is once again on the freedom of Jesus: he is totally in control. There is also the paradox that he who came to give water such that those who drank of it would never be thirsty again (Jn 4:14), now cries out, 'I am thirsty.'

Verse 30 is saying that Jesus gave his spirit back to the Father; but it also means that he gave his spirit to those he was leaving behind.

Gospel Prayer

'*We all wish to be God with God, but there are few of us who want to live as men and women with his humanity, or to bear his cross with him and to be crucified with him in order to pay for the sins of the world.*' – Hedwidge of Brabant, 12th century mystic

Lord, there comes a time in life when people take charge of us:
– we become feeble through sickness or old age;
– we are confused or discouraged and must seek help;
– we feel overwhelmed by our sins.
Naturally we resent this and even refuse it.
Help us rather to enter freely into your will for us, carrying our own cross as Jesus did, even if we must go out of the city to the place of the skull.

'*If we want to live a perfect life, we have only to despise the things that Christ despised on the cross and to desire what Christ desired.*' – St Thomas Aquinas

Lord, forgive us for being concerned about what is secondary, what people think of us, what company we keep or whether we have succeeded.
Teach us to be more like Jesus,
unconcerned that we are crucified and between two thieves, one on either side with us in the middle,
but so clear in our commitments that a notice could be fixed over us stating what we stand for and no one could deny it.

'*We should never allow our divisions to become tolerable or worse still comfortable. We should ever recognise the scandal that Anglicans and Catholics must celebrate two Eucharists to make one memorial on the Day of the Lord.*' – Archbishop Runcie before Pope John Paul II, October 1989

Lord, as Jesus was dying on the cross, the soldiers divided his clothing into four shares,
but his priestly garment they left seamless, woven in one piece from neck to hem.
We pray that very soon, when our churches celebrate the memory of that day, we may experience that he has kept all his followers one.

'The only thing I can boast of is the cross of our Lord Jesus Christ.' – Gal 6:14
Lord, forgive for distancing ourselves as church from the radical stance of Jesus
settling for compromise and the safe way.
But once like Mary we remain near the cross of Jesus,
his true disciples will recognise the church as their mother
 and will make a place for her in their homes.

'Our concern is for fidelity not success.' – Mother Teresa
Lord, we pray for the grace to come to the end of our lives as Jesus came to the end of his,
knowing that everything we had to do has now been completed,
that what has been written about us in the scriptures has been perfectly fulfilled,
so that we can say, 'it is accomplished', bow our heads and give peacefully back to you the spirit you breathed into us.

'Our Jesuits sought a peace built on the rights of the poor. Their death will surely be the seed of new commitments for peace in this country.' – The Provincial Superior of the six Jesuits killed in El Salvador, November 1989
Lord, we thank you for those who die like Jesus faithful to their vision,
and so hand over their spirit to live on in others.

Holy Saturday

Gospel Reading Mk 16:1-7
¹When the sabbath was over, Mary of Magdala, Mary the mother of James, and Salome, brought spices with which to go and anoint him. ²And very early in the morning on the first day of the week they went to the tomb, just as the sun was rising.
³They had been saying to one another, 'Who will roll away the stone for us from the entrance to the tomb?' ⁴But when they looked they could see that the stone – which was very big – had already been rolled back. ⁵On entering the tomb they saw a young man in a white robe seated on the right-hand side, and they were struck with amazement. ⁶But he said to them, 'There is no need for alarm. You are looking for Jesus of Nazareth, who was crucified: he has risen, he is not here. See, here is the place where they laid him. ⁷But you must go and tell his disciples and Peter, "He is going before you to Galilee; it is there you will see him, just as he told you."'

Meditation

The gospel reading for the Easter Vigil this year is St Mark's account of the resurrection of Jesus.

Each gospel has its own account of this central moment in the life of Jesus. Concentrate on the text before you, not on other accounts you may be more familiar with. St Mark tells the story from the perspective of the women who went to the tomb but you can also read it from the perspective of the disciples who, in contrast, remained indoors and received the good news from them.

You should divide the story as follows:
Verses 1-2: the women are symbols of faithful watching. Note

the symbolism of 'the first day of the week' and 'the sun was rising'.

Verses 3-4: the problem of the stone in front of the tomb is very symbolic.

Verses 5-6: the words of the young man in the white robe express the mystery of the empty tomb. Enter into the dramatic contrast between the attitude of the women and the reality of the risen Jesus.

Verse 7 is the commission given to the women. In this account there is no question of an appearance of Jesus in Jerusalem. Ask yourself what is the significance of the disciples returning to Galilee where the great adventure started.

Gospel Prayer

Lord, we thank you for faithful people:
– friends who stay with us even when we let them down;
– members of our parish who persevere in the community in times of discord;
– those in our movement who are not discouraged by corruption and betrayal within it;
– people in the Middle East who continue to work for peace.
Whereas most of us looked on past hopes as dead and gone, they, like the women at the tomb of Jesus, continued to mourn for what they had lost.
So they were there when a new day dawned and the sun rose, and they were able to announce to us who had lost hope, the good news that it was the first day of a new beginning.

Lord we remember a time when we were in some bondage:
– we were in the grip of some addiction;
– our family life was in deep crisis;
– unemployment had us totally discouraged.

Now looking back, we remember how we worried about what turned out to be no problem at all:
– what our friends would say;
– how one particular child would respond;
– whether our health would stand up to work.
We were like the women on Easter morning asking themselves who would roll away the great stone from the entrance to the tomb, when the moment of grace had already come and the stone was quite irrelevant to their situation. Thank you, Lord.

'Walk the dark ways of faith and you will attain the vision of God.'– St Augustine
Lord, forgive us for continuing to focus on the past:
– we harp on wrongs done to us by parents or teachers;
– we regret mistakes we made, opportunities we missed;
– we want to prove we are better than others;
– we try to rebuild relationships that have ended;
– we resent getting old or sickly.
Send us someone like the young man in the white robe who spoke to the women at the tomb of Jesus,
to tell us that crucifixion is not the end,
we must not look for Jesus in a tomb because he has risen, he is not there.
Your will is that we go back to Galilee to resume our lives because he is going before us there and it is there that we will see him just as he told us.

'All nations have opportunities which they may grasp if only they can summon up the courage and the will.' – Sir Arthur Lewis, West Indian economist
Lord, there are nations today which are trapped in an endless cycle of racial, ethnic, or religious conflict,
the Middle East, Ireland, Sri Lanka, South Africa.
We thank you for the women of those nations,
who like Mary of Magdala, Mary the Mother of James, and

Salome, have seen with their own eyes that life cannot be con-
tained in a tomb,
and have gone to tell their leaders that they must move forward
to new places where they will find life just as you told them.

Lord, sometimes the good news of resurrection from the dead
is so overpowering that all we can do is to run away, frightened out of our wits, and even though we have a wonderful
message to transmit, for a long time we can say nothing to a
soul.